YOUR KNOWLEDGE HAS VALUE

- We will publish your bachelor's and master's thesis, essays and papers

- Your own eBook and book - sold worldwide in all relevant shops

- Earn money with each sale

Upload your text at www.GRIN.com and publish for free

Making heart diseases detectable. The invention of an algorithm for systematically predictions

Daniyal Baig

Bibliographic information published by the German National Library:

The German National Library lists this publication in the National Bibliography; detailed bibliographic data are available on the Internet at http://dnb.dnb.de.

ISBN: 9783346297631
This book is also available as an ebook.

© GRIN Publishing GmbH
Nymphenburger Straße 86
80636 München

Print and binding: Books on Demand GmbH, Norderstedt, Germany
Printed on acid-free paper from responsible sources.

The present work has been carefully prepared. Nevertheless, authors and publishers do not incur liability for the correctness of information, notes, links and advice as well as any printing errors.

GRIN web shop: https://www.grin.com/document/953437

Efficient Heart disease prediction system using machine learning

Muhammad Daniyal Baig

Department of Computer Science Lahore garrison university, Dha Phase 6, Lahore

Table of contents

Abstract 3

Introduction.. 4

Heart disease 5

Literature review 5

Proposed Algorithm 6

    Classification... 7

    Data set 7

    Heart UCI Dataset.. 8

Used Prediction models 10

    Naive Bayes 10

    K nearest neighbor 10

    Decision tree.. 11

    Random forest.. 11

    Experimentation Results 11

Conclusion 13

References... 14

Abstract

In today's world the heart disease is increasing. Hence a lot of data related to the heart disease is being collected by using data mining. This important can be evaluated and used to predict and detect the coronary artery disease and heart related problem before the occurrence of the fatal experience. In our research paper we will conduct and experimental analysis to seek an improved method to predict heart disease in the upcoming years. So efficient steps can be taken in order to predict and treat the avoidable fatal heart problem. We will be creating an efficient algorithm which will detect the disease on the basis of some parameters and give as much accurate information as possible. By using our method you can systematically predict the risk of suffering from this disease. The main feature utilized in the detection will include age, gender, max heart rate, exercise induced angina etc.

Keywords: *Machine learning, data mining, supervised learning algorithms, Heart disease prediction.*

Introduction

Many different types of life threating diseases are amongst us but heart disease has been studied the most in medical research. Early diagnosis of the disease is a very difficult task. We want to introduce an automated way of prediction of heart disease in individuals. This solution is not one and all solution but it will serve as a complementary diagnosis in the field of medical research. The main task in heart disease is to detect the disease early and treat it efficiently before any fatal experience occurs.

Many techniques are used to detect the heart problem for example EKG, ECG; Echo monitoring these are the devices which are used for diagnosing the disease. Several factors play a major role in the increased risk of getting this disease. Obesity, lack of exercise, high blood pressure and high cholesterol all increase the risk of heart problems.

As the digital technology is rapidly growing a lot of data is available throughout the world. Often poor diagnosis can cause serious harm to the patient. Detecting disease on time is one of the major aspects of our system. Around 17 million deaths occur due to heart disease and strokes. Mental stress and physical stress also contribute to the increase in heart disease. But the diagnosis costs a lot for the everyday person even in the developed countries.

Many people cannot afford the treatment and the diagnosis test. Hence an automated system will be created which will use provided historical data in order to diagnose heart disease for everyone. Mainly our system will work as a support system rather than a full time diagnosing system. Our system will help the doctors to detect the disease on time and predict heart problems for younger people. So, effective steps can be taken in order to resolve this issue.

Heart disease

Heart is an organ of the body. It works as a pump; it supplies blood to all the other parts of the body. The human is dependent on the circulation of blood from the heart. Life is dependent on the efficient working of the heart.

Many factors play role in increasing chances of heart disease:

1) Smoking
2) Family history
3) Obesity
4) High blood pressure
5) Physical inactivity

While detecting the disease through machine learning algorithms mostly these parameters are kept in mind. As these parameters are important factors in increase anyone's chances in acquiring this problem.

Literature review

Heart disorder (HD) is one among the most not unusual sicknesses today, due to variety of contributing elements, like excessive strain level, diabetes, sterol fluctuation, exhaustion and masses of others. companion diploma early diagnosing of such un wellness has been probe for numerous years, and masses of expertise analytics equipment are carried out to help fitness care providers to pick out some of the primary symptoms and symptoms of HD. numerous exams are frequently executed on capability sufferers to require the extra precautions measures to cut back the effect of having the sort of unwellness [1], and dependable techniques to are expecting early levels of HD, just like the techniques proposed throughout this paper, are frequently a critical challenge for saving lives. variety of Machine Learning (ML) algorithms, such as, Naïve mathematician, random Gradient Descents (SGD), Support Vector Machine (SVM), K- Nearest Neighbor (K-NN), Adaboost, JRip, name tree J48, et al had been carried out for the goal of category and prediction of HD dataset, and masses of promising consequences had been given inside the literature [2]. Due to the complex nature of the HD, suggested exams, that must be prioritized [3], and projected strategies want to be selected rigorously, anyplace authors labored on appropriately and with performance are expecting coronary heart-associated hospitalizations supported the available patient-precise anamnesis, and five gadget studying algorithms, specifically SVM, AdaBoost, deliver regression, a naïve mathematician occasion classifier anyplace used, and consequences confirmed had been constant for all used classifiers for accomplishable prediction accuracy with a detection fee of 80 two. Authors in [4] projected companion diploma algorithmic rule to are expecting the lifestyles of coronary heart disorder exploitation Back Propagation MLP (Multilayer Perceptron) of Artificial Neural Network on a given HD dataset classifications, and cubic centimeter algorithms, mainly neural networks for the postulation of HD instances become hired in [5], anyplace authors projected to broaden companion diploma software which may also are expecting the vulnerability of a cardiovascular disorder given simple signs like age, sex, pulse fee, and neural networks confirmed the most accurate and dependable algorithmic rule for the projected device. a expertise mining version has been developed [6] exploitation Random Forest classifier to decorate the prediction accuracy and to research numerous occasions related to cardiovascular disorder, and experimental consequences confirmed that category exploitation Random Forest Classification algorithmic rule are frequently with achievement hired in predicting the occasions and threat elements related to HD.

Proposed Algorithm

In our system the main task is to predict how many people will get heart disease or not on the basis of the historical data available. Our architecture will work on a top to bottom approach. Heart disease dataset will be downloaded. Than the missing values from the dataset will be extracted. After dataset preprocessing the dataset will be divided into 0 and 1 format. When no heart disease will be detected the results will display 0 and 1 will be displayed for positivity of the heart disease.

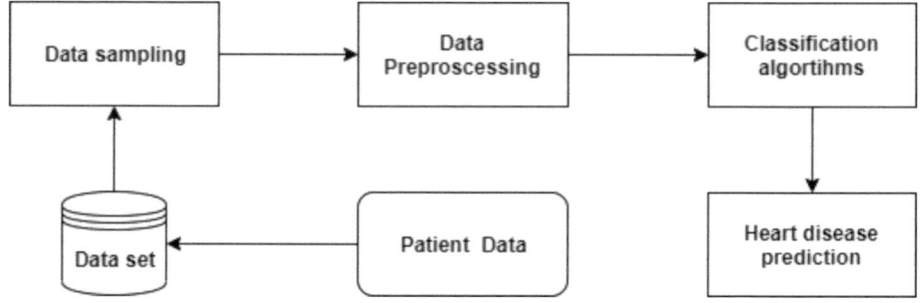

Figure 1. Proposed model (author own created)

Classification

Heart disease prediction is basically a classification or a clustering algorithmic problem. We performed data dimensionality on the dataset, so more perceive data is only used to make better and accurate predictions. We will be preforming the machine learning algorithms four algorithms.

1)   Naïve Bayes

2)   K- nearest neighbor

3)   Decision Tree

4)   Random forest

Data set

In order to remove biasness and skewedness from the data the data set needs to be preprocessed. It is a necessity to preprocess the dataset for the effective utilization. The dataset is divided into training and testing dataset for accurate predictions. Preprocessing mostly adapts the missing values, standard scalar and robust scalar will be adopted to remove the unutilized values from the data set. Any value which is missing from the data set gets deleted by using these techniques. Standard scalar makes sure that values 0 and 1 variance.

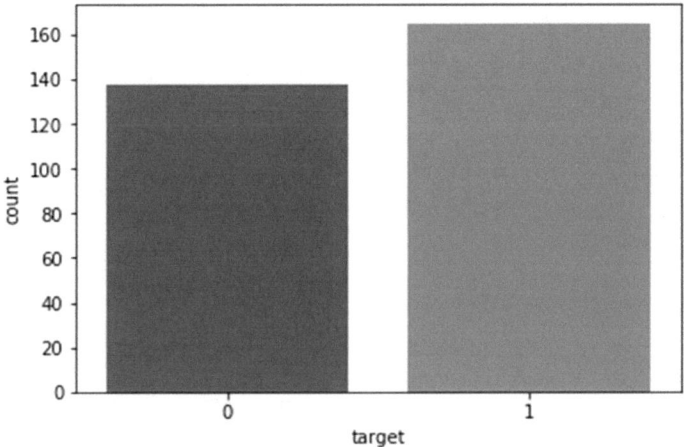

Figure 1 Dataset division (author own created)

The dataset is divided into 0 and 1. Total value of 1 is 165. 1 represents the people with heart disease and the 0 is 138. 0 represents the value of people not having the heart disease.

Heart UCI Dataset

Heart Disease Dataset in particular is called the Cleveland dataset is mostly used for machine learning research. The dataset contains 76 attributes but out of the 76 attributes 14 are specifically used for diagnosis in a systematic manner.

- **Feature Extraction**

Any new feature is extracted from the available original set of features. Principal component analysis (PCA) is utilized to extract the subset features from the data set. The best reconstruction is provided by PCA algorithm.

8

- **Data set Features**
- age - age in years

- sex - sex(1 = male; 0 = female)

- chest_pain - chest pain type (1 = typical angina; 2 = atypical angina; 3 = non-angina pain; 4 = asymptomatic)

- blood_pressure - resting blood pressure (in mm Hg on admission to the hospital)

- serum_cholestoral - serum cholesterol in mg/dl

- fasting_blood_sugar - fasting blood sugar > 120 mg/dl (1 = true; 0 = false)

- electrocardiographic - resting electrocardiographic results (0 = normal; 1 = having ST-T; 2 = hypertrophy)

- max_heart_rate - maximum heart rate achieved
- induced_angina - exercise induced angina (1 = yes; 0 = no)

- ST_depression - ST depression induced by exercise relative to rest

---

- slope - the slope of the peak exercise ST segment (1 = upsloping; 2 = flat; 3 = downsloping)

- no_of_vessels - number of major vessels (0-3) colored by flourosopy

---

- thal - 3 = normal; 6 = fixed defect; 7 = reversable defect

- diagnosis - the predicted attribute - diagnosis of heart disease (angiographic disease status) (Value 0 = < 50% diameter narrowing; Value 1 = > 50% diameter narrowing)

Types of features

There are 3 types of main features used in the dataset. They are as follows:

Categorical features (Has two or more categories and each value in that feature can be categorised by them): **sex,**	(Has two or more categories and each value in that feature can be categorised by them): **gender, chest_pain age, blood _pressure, serum_cholestoral, max_heart_rate, ST_depression**
Ordinal features	**fasting_blood_sugar, electrocardiographic, induced_angina, slope, no_of_vessels, thal, diagnosis**
Continuous features	Variable taking values between any two points or between the minimum or maximum values in the feature column):

Feature table no 1

Used Prediction models

Naive Bayes

Naive Bayes is a classification algorithm which is based on Bayes theorem. It is a supervised learning algorithm. The basic assumption in naïve Bayes is that assumption of features is independent of each other. It is very fast, highly scalable.

K nearest neighbor

KNN algorithm classifies on the basis of similarity measures. It classifies new cases on the similarity measure of the previous available cases. It is basically used in pattern recognition and estimation process. It is a supervised learning algorithm. It learns from the past experiences. It can be implemented in both classification and regression problems.

Decision tree

Decision tree is a supervised learning algorithm. It is a classification algorithm used both for regression analysis and classifications problems. The goal of decision tree is to create a model that predicts the value of a target variable by learning simple decision rules inferred from the data features

Random forest

Random forest is a classification model used for classification and regression analysis. In random forest multiple decision trees are created. In random forest the best features are selected amongst the random features. It basically used bagging and feature randomness to create a tree.

Experimentation Results

Algorithm	Accuracy
Naïve Bayes	86 %
KNN	65%
Decision Tree	82%
Random Forest	94%

Table No. 2 Experimental results

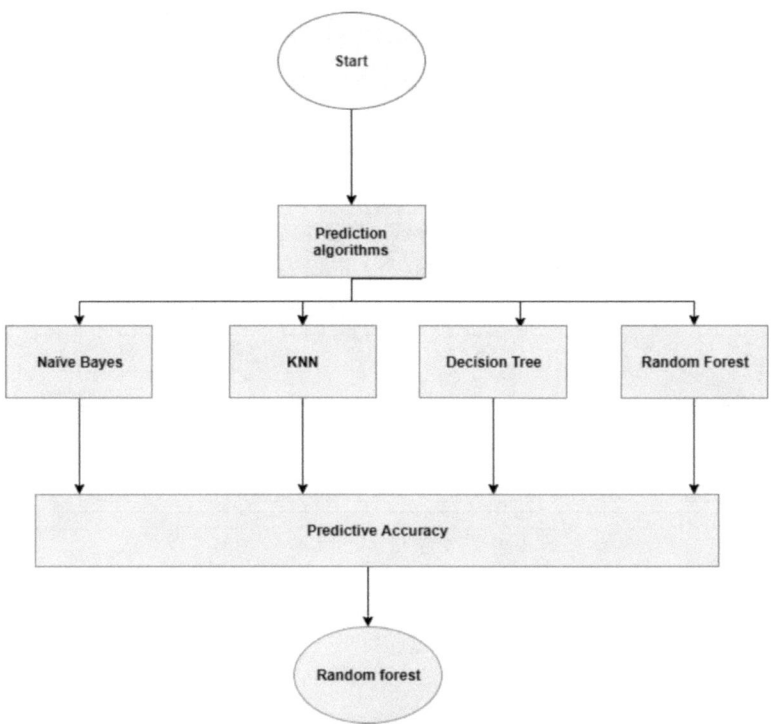

Figure 2. Predictive analysis (author own created)

Conclusion

In the research study we performed a machine learning approach to predict the heart disease. The system was implemented on four algorithms using the Cleveland dataset for heart disease. The algorithms used were Naïve Bayes, KNN, Decision tree and random forest. KNN algorithm provided the least accuracy of about 65 percent, while the naïve bayes and decision tree gae 86 percent and 82 percent accuracy. On the other hand the random forest algorithm displayed an accuracy of 94 percent which is optimal solution in order to predict the heart disease efficiently.

References

[1] "The Atlas of Heart Disease and Stroke", [online]. http://www.who.int/cardiovascular_diseases/res ources/atlas/en/

[2] J. S. Rumsfeld, K. E. Joynt, and T. M. Maddox, "Big data analytics to improve cardiovascular care: promise and challenges", Nature Reviews Cardiology, Vol.13, No.6, pp.350, 2016.

[3] W. Dai, T. S. Brisimi, W. G. Adams, T. Mela, V. Saligrama, and I. C. Paschalidis, "Prediction of hospitalization due to heart diseases by supervised learning methods", International Journal of Medical Informatics, Vol.84, No.3, pp.189–197, 2015.

[4] I. Kamkar, M. Akbarzadeh-T and M. Yaghoobi, "Intelligent water drops a new optimization algorithm for solving the Vehicle Routing Problem", In: Proc. of IEEE International Conference on Systems, Man and Cybernetics, pp.4142-4146, 2010.

[5] N. M. Gazzaz, M. K. Yusoff, M. F. Ramli, H. Juahir, and A. Z. Aris, "Artificial neural network modeling of the water quality index using land use areas as predictors", Water Environment Research, Vol.87, No.2, pp.99- 112, 2015.

[6] Y. Zhang, S. Wang, and G. Ji, "A comprehensive survey on particle swarm optimization algorithm and its applications", Received: October 22, 2018 252 International Journal of Intelligent Engineering and Systems, Vol.12, No.1, 2019 DOI: 10.22266/ijies2019.0228.24 Mathematical Problems in Engineering, Vol.2015, Article ID 931256, 38 pages, 2015.

[7] H. M. Alshamlan, G. H. Badr and Y. A. Alohali, "Genetic Bee Colony (GBC) algorithm: A new gene selection method for microarray cancer classification", Computational Biology and Chemistry, Vol.56, pp.49-60, 2015.

[8] L. Yu, and H. Liu, "Feature selection for highdimensional data: A fast correlation-based filter solution", In: Proc. of the 20th International Conference on Machine Learning, pp. 856-863, 2003.

[9] M. Fatima and M. Pasha, "Survey of machine learning algorithms for disease diagnostic. Journal of Intelligent Learning Systems and Applications", Journal of Intelligent Learning Systems and Applications, Vol.9, No.01, pp.1, 2017.

[10] K. C. Tan, E. J. Teoh, Q. Yu, and K. C. Goh, "A hybrid evolutionary algorithm for attribute selection in data mining", Expert Systems with Applications, Vol.36, No.4, pp.8616-8630, 2009.

[11] A. F. Otoom, E. E. Abdallah, Y. Kilani, A. Kefaye, and M. Ashour, "Effective diagnosis and

monitoring of heart disease", International Journal of Software Engineering and Its Applications, Vol.9, No.1, pp. 143-156, 2015.

[12] G. Parthiban and S. K. Srivatsa, "Applying machine learning methods in diagnosing heart disease for diabetic patients", International Journal of Applied Information Systems, Vol.3, No.7, pp.2249-0868, 2012.

[13] V. Chaurasia and S. Pal, "Data mining approach to detect heart diseases", International Journal of Advanced Computer Science and Information Technology, Vol.2, No.4, pp.56-66, 2014.

[14] K. Vembandasamy, R. Sasipriya, and E. Deepa, "Heart Diseases Detection Using Naive Bayes Algorithm", IJISET-International Journal of Innovative Science, Engineering & Technology, Vol.2, pp.441-444, 2015.

[15] X. Liu, X. Wang, Q. Su, M. Zhang, Y.Zhu, Q. Wang, and Q. Wang, "A hybrid classification system for heart disease diagnosis based on the rfrs method", Computational and Mathematical Methods in Medicine, Vol.2017, Article ID 8272091, 11 pages, 2017.

[16] A. Malav, K. Kadam, and P. Kamat, "Prediction of heart disease using k-means and artificial neural network as a hybrid approach to improve accuracy", International Journal of Engineering and Technology, Vol.9, No.4, 2017.